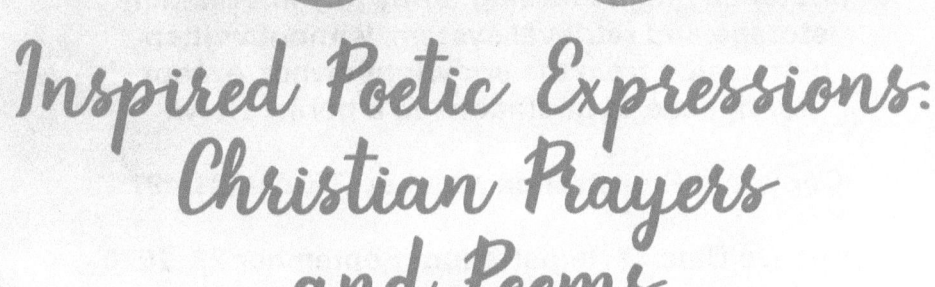

Inspired Poetic Expressions: Christian Prayers and Poems

S. LAUREEN BROWN

Inspired Poetic Expressions:
Christian Prayers and Poems

Copyright © 2020 by S. Laureen Brown

All rights reserved. No parts of this book may be reproduced or transmitted in any form or any means, electronic or mechanical, including photocopying, recording, or by any information storage and retrieval system, without written permission from the copyright owner, except for the use of quotations in a book review.

Copyright Registration Number: TXu 2-221-497

Effective Date of Registration: September 23, 2020

Library of Congress Control Number: 2020920403

ISBN: 978-0-578-77896-9

Published by S. Laureen Brown

Contact information: slaureenbrown@icloud.com

Printed in the United States of America

To the God of all creation
for the gifts He has given me.
To my Lord and Savior Jesus Christ,
thank you for saving me.

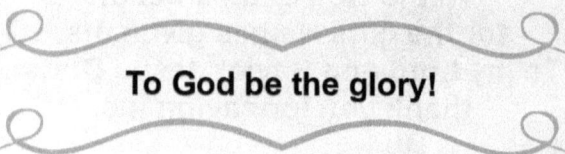

To God be the glory!

Table of Contents

Prayer Poems...7
A Mother's Prayer..8
Fill My Empty Cup..9
Daily Bread...10
A Woman's Prayer..11
Lesson Learned..12
Confidence in Christ..14
A Drug Addict's Prayer..15
The Overcoming Prayer...17
Here Am I, Send Me, I Will Go.................................18

Christian Poems..19
Never Lose Hope...20
Already Won...22
Beauty of the Sea...23
Better Days...24
Called to Lead (For Pastor Walton)............................25
Choose Your Lane..26
God Almighty..28
Grace and Mercy...29
He Will Forever Be..30
Jesus Came..31
Jesus Is on the Way...32
Keeper of the Book..33
Living Testimony..34
Look for Tomorrow...35
Memo from God to the Church...................................36

More Than I Deserve	38
Pray	39
Remember the Call	40
Rescued	41
Struggling	43
Woman of Favor	45
You Can Make It	46
He Will Be Your Light	47
Oh, The Joy I Have	49
Praise the Creator	50
The Greatest Gift of All	51
Willing Vessel	52
The Treasures of Your Heart ... Where Are They?	53
Taming the Tongue	55
Women Striving for Excellence in Times Like These	56
Now That I'm Saved	58
Don't Throw in the Towel	59
In Times Like These We Need a Savior	60
Breaking Up Our Fallow Ground Is Hard to Do	62
River of Life	64
Changed	65
Let Go and Leave the Past Behind	67
Reminders from Our Heavenly Father	68
Forgiveness	70
Commit to the Harvest	71
Please Keep Walking in Your Deliverance	72
Sistah Saint	73
Preparation for Spiritual Warfare	75
The Final Call (Selah)	77
The Most High God	78

Prayer Poems

A Mother's Prayer

Oh Lord, how I need thee,
Pour out your spirit on me.
Give me strength to make it through,
Show me what I need to do.
Trouble is brewing and it is all around,
I am struggling hard to keep from falling down.
My flesh is weak and my soul is faint,
Lord, please refresh your weary saint.
I feel like I've done all I can,
Now I need your help just to stand.
My children are being bombarded by the enemy's fire,
But I know that the devil is a deceiving liar.
"No weapon formed against me shall prosper"
is written in your holy word,
Please open my kids' eyes
because their vision is blurred.
Save them Lord before it is too late,
Don't let hell be their eternal fate.
Shield them from every fiery dart,
Give them the mind to accept you
and a brand-new start.
Father, you gave me these children
and I dedicated them back to you,
Please stop everything that the devil has set out to do.
I'm fasting and praying, as my soul cries out to you,
I'm trusting that you will see my children through.
In the name of your precious son Jesus,
I ask these things of you.
Amen.

Fill My Empty Cup

My soul is empty, it longs to be filled.
My spirit is broken, it needs to be healed.
I'm like a bird with clipped wings, struggling to get up.
I'm holding in my hand an almost empty cup.
I feel like a lost child, anxious to be found,
Alone in a big world just wandering around.
Lord, please saturate my soul
with your everlasting love,
Mend my broken spirit with your mercy from above.
Father, I believe that You love me
more than I will ever know,
And as You fill my cup with Your grace,
please let it overflow.

Daily Bread

Grant me Lord my daily bread,
And a place to lay my head.
I do not need worldly wealth,
Just a reasonable portion of strength and health.
I do not have to drive a fancy car,
And do not want to be a movie star.
Oh Lord, with all that said,
Grant me this, my daily bread.
All I want is what I need,
Lord, with You I will succeed.
Fame and fortune would be nice,
But that all comes with too big a price.
Give me just enough and nothing more,
Please keep me Lord from being poor.
Oh Lord, with all that said,
Grant me this, my daily bread.
Nothing more and nothing less,
I want your joy, peace, and happiness.
Your daily bread gets me by,
Just like the manna that fell from the sky.
You are the shepherd who supplies all my needs,
I'm blessed because of your merciful deeds.
Oh Lord, with all that said,
Grant me this, my daily bread.

A Woman's Prayer

In my secret closet I come to you in prayer,
Daily Heavenly Father, I want to meet you there.
I fast some days and push away my plate,
And tune everything out as I seek your face.
Guidance and deliverance will surely be given,
But I can't half-step with my Christian way of living.
Ninety-nine and a half certainly will not do,
Lord, help me to give one hundred percent to you.
Help me when things and people get on my last nerve,
Gently remind me that it is
my duty to love and to serve.
Help me as I profess to be called by your name,
To unify with my sisters in Christ
with honor and not shame.
Father, I give you praise, honor, and glory too,
In the name of Jesus, I ask these things of You.
Let every redeemed woman of the Lord say Amen!
Amen.

Lesson Learned

Lord, please help me to stand,
Please reach out your hand.
Grab me before I fall,
Listen to me as I call.
I've collided with trouble,
I'm in need of help.
This thing is something new,
Lord, I don't know what to do.
The enemy thinks he's already won,
But I know it's not over until you say it is done.
I need a resolution to this situation,
I'm crying out in complete desperation.
Have mercy Lord, please show me the way,
I need help right now, this minute, please don't delay.
My life could very well end,
On You I do depend.
Help from anyone else just won't do,
Lord, no one can help me but You.
There's irony to this unfolding drama,
I should have listened to my mama.
She told me he was no good,
Lord, you told her and she understood.
But I was infatuated and did not want to see,
Just what the man was doing to me.
I was on a slide rapidly going down,
It would not be long before I reached the ground.

Caught in a world of trouble fighting for my life,
Being abused by a man who asked me to be his wife.
I prayed *Lord, please don't let me die,*
While in a state of shock asking myself why.
That very moment it all came back to me,
It was picture-perfect clear to see.
All hope was gone and the light grew dim,
Lord, I turned my back on You
and chose to be with him.
Father, forgive me for my sins, I was wrong,
I gave in to my flesh when I should have stayed strong.
Now Satan has my back hard-pressed against the wall,
Laughing at me, saying now he's in control of it all.
Then you reminded me that
You will never leave or forsake me,
So, from the depths of my soul
I shouted please make the devil flee.
Then not more than a second passed,
You strengthened me to break loose
and to get away fast.
Before this all went down,
you warned me over and over again,
But like a paper clip to a magnet, I was drawn to sin.
Looking back, I wish that I had
listened and not taken the wrong turn,
Lord, I sincerely thank You for sparing my life
and for the lesson I learned.

Confidence in Christ

Lord, you hear every word I say,
I give my troubles to You while I kneel and pray.
Too much for me to handle,
More than I can bear.
I bring them to your altar,
And I will leave them there.
I trust You'll work them out,
For You know what's best for me.
Your perfect will shall be done,
What You allow is what shall surely be.

A Drug Addict's Prayer

Dear God,
I've been on drugs for a very long time,
And my drug use led me to a life of crime.
I have done things that I should not have done,
A couple of incidents involved the use of a gun.
I have not been a father to my kids,
I wonder can they forgive me for the things I did.
I abused their mother time and time again,
The last time it was so bad, I was sent to the pen.
I stole from my mother and
other members of my family,
I know they could never trust me.
I sunk to the lowest depths of this life,
Drugs only caused me troubles and strife.
I want to change, but I don't know how,
I need you to help me right now.
No one wants anything to do with me,
I am as low as I could be.
I've been told that you could make me new,
I don't know why you would want to.

I told you just how bad I've been,
Why would you forgive my sins?
How could you love someone like me?
I've become a reject of this society.
I was brought up the right way,
But I chose to go astray.
God, I always believed that you were there,
But honestly, I did not care.
I tried to get as far away from you as I could,
I couldn't associate myself with anything good.
Suddenly I can see the error of my ways,
That's why I'm calling on you today.
I want to start my life anew,
So, I give myself to you.
I know that I have to reap all that I have sown,
But I can make it through
as long as you never leave me alone.
I pray this prayer with a humble heart,
Hoping that you will give me a new start.
I ask you this in the name of Jesus.
Amen.

The Overcoming Prayer

I want to be a Romans 12 saint,
But sometimes I feel like I just can't.
Bless those who hate on me?
Or do good to those who have done me wrong?
I confess, I am weak in those areas;
Lord, please make me strong.
Help me to overcome evil with good,
I want to live how the Holy Scriptures
says that I should.
When I want to handle things my own way,
Gently remind me Lord that
Vengeance is Yours to repay.
I want to be transformed and
leave the cares of this world behind,
Lord, please help me daily to renew my mind.
Help me to stay focused on you,
As I do what you have called me to do.
I want to be invisible so that You are who people see,
When I exercise this gift you have given me.
In the body of Christ, help me to cheerfully do my part,
To serve others with a Christ-like heart.
Help me adhere to Your perfect plan,
Help me to never let go of Your unfailing hand.
In the name of Jesus, I pray.
Amen.

Here Am I, Send Me, Lord I Will Go

I can't change the world but I can do my part,
I stand before you Lord with a willing heart.
In obedience I'll spread your word to all whom I can,
Everyone has to hear about your salvation plan.
There is work to be done, this I do know,
Here am I, send me, Lord I will go.
I'll go only where you tell me to go.
I'll say only what you tell me to say.
I will walk in your will and not my own.
I commit my renewed self to you, the old me is gone.
There is work to be done, this I do know,
Here am I, send me, Lord I will go.
Trials and tribulations, I'm sure to face,
But that won't deter me from finishing this race.
My mind is made up and my vision is clear,
I'll listen to your directions with attentive ears.
There is work to be done, this I do know,
Here am I, send me, Lord I will go.
I've been in the wilderness and you led me out,
"Victory is mine through Christ Jesus"
is now what I proclaim and shout.
The world needs to know that all things
are possible with you.
I can't keep it to myself any longer;
sinners need to know the truth too.
There is work to be done, this I do know,
Here am I, send me, Lord I will go.

Never Lose Hope

The devil is trying to take control,
he wants our children to steal their souls.
Blatantly and boldly he is tightening his hold.
Our children can't spiritually see
the devil's intent of trickery.
He wants them to misbehave as he
slowly pushes them to an early grave.
He desires our children in their youth
so he can shield them from the truth.
The truth is God is all our children need,
with the Lord they can succeed.
God can help them to excel and
save them from a burning hell,
God can mend shattered hearts and
give anyone a brand-new start.
Through these confusing and
troublesome adolescent years,
God can provide comfort and wipe away the tears.
The devil is trying to take their minds,
It's time we saints press rewind.

Go back and stand on God's word,
The idea of the devil taking our children is absurd.
We are children of the King of kings,
Lord and Creator of everything.
In the name of Jesus, Satan must flee,
This is just how it has to be.
Our children are gifts to us from the Lord,
We can't let the devil push them overboard.
It's time we saints take a stand and
join together hand in hand.
We have to pray continuously and
thank God in advance for victory.
Our children may seem to be sliding
on a downward slope,
But we have to trust in God and never lose hope.
Our prayers are not going unheard,
God hears our every word.
The foundation has already been paved,
Our children will be spirit-filled and saved.
They'll make it if we pray them through,
We can't give up no matter what they do.

Already Won

Satan is busy doing what he does best,
He's pulled out his big guns, now I face a test.
Now that I'm living right, he wants me to fail,
He wants to take my soul and sentence it to hell.
But I've been redeemed; Jesus' blood paid the price.
Now I have power from on high
because of the Savior's sacrifice.
No matter how many fiery darts
the devil throws my way,
I know the Lord will see me through
each and every day.
The storm winds may be blowing,
but they will have to pass,
I'm staying with the Lord no matter
how long the storm lasts.
Satan will find the smallest crack to slip in,
but his presence will be revealed,
The Holy Spirit will not allow
Satan's tricks to be concealed.
If I resist the devil, he will flee,
He is no match for the Holy Spirit inside of me.
So, no matter what the devil is doing,
will do, or has already done,
I don't have to worry because the battle is already won.

Beauty of the Sea

As the ocean waves gently creep upon the white sand,
And darkness falls upon the land,
I sit on a beach in Monterey,
Praising God for a lovely day.
The fresh sea breeze is softly blowing through my hair,
I meditate as I breathe in the ocean air.
I feel calmness coming over me,
As I sit there by the sea.
Oh, what a marvelous sight to behold,
A body of water so mesmerizing,
majestic, and yet so old.
Created by the true and living God,
I sit in silence,
In the distance, the ocean seems
as if it touches the sky,
It goes much further than I can view with my naked eye.
The sun looks as if it is sinking into the sea,
I am entranced as I stare at nature's beauty.
To some this may sound very odd,
But sunsets at the beach is where I feel closest to God.
I am captivated by the wonders
of God's marvelous might,
As the darkness slowly chases away the sunlight.

Better Days

So many obstacles in my way,
I find it hard to face each day.
So weak from the struggle, my soul feels faint,
I want to give up but I just can't.
I remind myself that a change will someday come,
And remember where my help comes from.
Jesus is my sustainer in the midst of it all,
He strengthens me when I am about to fall.
The enemy thinks that he has the upper hand,
But God has given me the power to stand.
This trouble cannot last too long,
Even in my weakness I'll proclaim that I am strong.
I rejoice in advance with a heart filled with praise,
Thanking God Almighty for better days.

Called to Lead
(For Pastor Walton)

Your calling was confirmed before you ever existed,
You knew it to be true although you resisted.
It took a few years for you to totally surrender,
You wanted to be real and not a holy pretender.
You sold out completely
when you accepted Jesus the Savior,
You changed your walk, your talk,
and your worldly behavior.
Even though times were tough, you never turned back,
You purposed in your heart to stay on God's track.
God called you to pastor your own congregation,
Humbly you submitted without hesitation.
Your first church was neither great nor grand,
You trusted in God and followed His plan.
God, you, your family, and a couple of friends,
Is all that was needed to make your church begin.
Faithful you've remained to the Lord's call,
You did not allow Satan to make you stumble or fall.
God has blessed you in more ways
than you could have ever dreamed,
Because you were steadfast
no matter how tough things seemed.
The Lord has allowed you to continuously succeed,
Because you are a pastor called by God to lead.

Choose Your Lane

It gets lonely in this straight and narrow lane,
I've seen a few travelers going my same way.
Some going at a steady pace,
Others passing by like they are in a timed race.
The pace doesn't matter because
the outcome is the same,
For those of us who stay till the end
on the straight and narrow lane.
We will see Jesus and worship at His throne,
All of our sorrows and pain will be forever gone.
The journey is not easy,
There is a struggle in every step.
But I made a promise to the Lord,
And that promise will be kept.
I vowed to go all the way and not to go astray,
In this straight and narrow lane
by God's grace I will stay.
To the left there is a lane that is wide and broad,
It has many travelers,
To me this seems so odd.

I see family members and friends,
They are going in the wrong direction, where
destruction and death are at the end.
I warn them, "You're going the wrong way!"
But they laugh at me and carry on,
They don't want to hear what I have to say.
They are deceived, blind, and under the devil's spell,
Wandering in darkness, unaware
that they are headed straight to hell.
Some have made it to the end of the lane
that is broad and wide,
And have paid the ultimate cost,
Their souls are forever lost.
Wake up! Open your eyes! Listen with attentive ears!
Jesus is soon to come, the end is certainly near.
Please don't delay, choose the right lane today.

God Almighty

Many people doubt that God lives,
Not realizing, while verbalizing their doubts,
That every breath they take He gives.
His might is written in the sky,
Better yet, it is evident in you and I.
Oh, how amazing is the creation of human beings,
When we look at ourselves,
it's God's likeness we are seeing.
With His words He spoke into existence the sun,
the stars, the moon, and the trees,
The heaven, the earth, the animals, and the seas.
He formed man from the land,
Because He has all power in his hands.
God breathed into Adam the breath of life,
And from man God created Eve, Adam's wife.
Almighty is God with all power in his hands,
Blessed are the people who heed God's plan.

Grace and Mercy

My life was full of troubles and woes,
But thank God for the grace and mercy he bestows.
If it had not been for the Lord on my side,
A few years ago, I would have surely died.
His grace and mercy kept me in my right mind,
Thank you Lord for being so kind.
If justice had its way, where would I be?
I'd certainly be damned eternally.
But God said, "I'll have mercy on you, my child,
Even while you're running wild.
Because I called you before
the foundations of the earth were laid,
The path you were to take was already made.
There were things you had to go through,
Before I could give my spirit to you."
I am where I'm supposed to be,
Only because of God's grace and mercy.

He Will Forever Be

God was, God is, and God will forever be
master and Lord of all.
We will never understand His mysterious ways,
It is futile to try, so just give Him praise.
Praise Him for all He has done,
God is God and He answers to no one.
He is just in all that He has done
and in all that He will do,
He does not have to explain anything to me or to you.
God is all-powerful, how wondrous is He,
He was, He is, and He will forever be.

Jesus Came

The stars did shine ever so bright,
On that holiest night of nights.
Into this world our savior was born,
With the glory of heaven, He was adorned.
Love became flesh in the person of Jesus Christ.
His mission was foretold prior to his birth,
He came to bring salvation to the people on earth.
His miraculous deeds are too numerous to count,
Jesus demonstrated what love was really about.
The time came for Him to depart,
But His earthly end was really a start.
Jesus removed the sting from death,
He arose and was filled with everlasting breath.
Although He left, He will return,
For that day my soul does yearn.
The world will never be the same,
Simply because Jesus came.
Praise His Holy Name.

Jesus Is on the Way!

It's time to get ready,
It's time to get your house in order,
Because time is winding down,
Seek the Lord, while He can be found.
Jesus is on the way!
No one knows the minute or the hour,
When Jesus will return with all power.
Jesus is Lord, every tongue will confess,
And every knee will bow at His holiness.
Who shall be able to stand?
Only those who accept God's plan.
The choice is yours to make,
Choose the Lord for your soul's sake.
Jesus is on the way!
So much trouble in the land,
How much more can the world stand?
The Bible is being fulfilled,
Because it's almost time
for Jesus Christ to be revealed.
Please don't harden your heart,
Today can be a new start.
The Lord is soon to return,
Your salvation should be your main concern.
Jesus is on the way!
No one knows the minute or the hour,
but it just might be today!

Keeper of the Book

There is a book still being written
since the beginning of time,
It chronicles the deeds of all mankind.
Everything done by you and me,
Will determine where we'll spend eternity.
There is still a chance while we are living,
To get things right and be forgiven.
For those who have passed, it's too late,
Death has already sealed their eternal fate.
Those who choose to live according to God's will,
Will rise from the dead when Christ is revealed.
Those who choose to go astray,
Will be condemned on Judgment Day.
The revelation of Jesus Christ is near,
Just look at the signs in the atmosphere.
Heed God's word when you hear it,
Humbly submit to God's spirit.
God is the keeper of the book,
He sits up high and down low He looks.
Recording everything that's done,
From the rising to the setting of each and everyone.

Living Testimony

Be a living Bible for the world to read,
Your shining light may be all a sinner needs,
To draw them to Jesus our Savior,
Simply by your Christ-like behavior.
Let your life be a living testimony.
Let the Holy Spirit that dwells in you,
Rays of light shine brightly through.
At times you don't have to say a word,
For the Holy Spirit to be heard.
Let your life be a living testimony.
You've been called and set apart,
God gave you His Spirit and cleaned your heart.
You've been born again,
Since God forgave you of your sins.
Let your life be a living testimony.
If your walk is new,
Your talk should be too.
Your life should not be the same,
If you've been changed in Jesus' name.
Let your life be a living testimony.
Stay on the right track,
Don't let anything pull you back.
Satan may try to tempt you,
Trust in God to see you through.
Let your life be a living testimony.
If you fall, don't wallow in sin,
Get up, repent, and keep moving.
Never be a hypocrite,
Let the Holy fire in you stay forever lit.
Let your life be a living testimony.

Look for Tomorrow

You may be in the middle of a storm,
And you feel physically and mentally worn.
You may feel that the pain is too much to bear,
And it seems like no one cares.
Look for tomorrow.
Depression has a tight hold on you,
You are in turmoil and do not know what to do.
Suicide is on your mind,
Because peace you cannot find.
Look for tomorrow.
Tomorrow is just a day away,
Hold on until tomorrow, you will be okay.
Do not make tonight your Judgment Day,
Life is precious; please do not take your own away.
Psalms 30:5b says, "Weeping may endure for a night,
but joy comes in the morning."
Hold on, don't give up, and don't give in.
Look for tomorrow.

Memo from God to the Church

So-called man and woman of God,
You grieve my spirit.
I gave you my word, but you refuse to read it.
My word tells you what you should and should not do,
But you act like it does not pertain to you.
You dishonor me by your deeds,
But you want me to supply all of your needs.
You acknowledge me only on Sundays,
And still you're too proud and
dignified to give me praise.
I hardly ever hear from you,
There are sinners who talk to me more than you do.
You call me only when things are bad,
Do you care if this makes me sad?
I've carried you through some life-changing situations,
Still you serve me with hesitation.
You give real saints a bad name,
Because you choose to play worldly games.
You lie, cheat, fornicate, commit adultery, and steal,
But you want people to believe you're real.

You won't even step out on faith and render your tithes,
But you struggle every month and you wonder why.
If you give to me, I will give to you,
Try it in faith and you'll see it's true.
Still there are some who have more than enough,
Those who ignore me and worship their stuff.
Under the blood-stained banner of my precious son,
Many wicked things in the church are being done.
There has to be a difference
between saints and sinners,
Or there will never be effective soul winners.
It's time for my saints to take a stand,
And adhere to every aspect of my commands.
Death is your wage for ungodly living,
Repent and you will be forgiven.
I love you and will never leave you,
Please stop letting Satan deceive you.

More Than I Deserve

God gives me all that I need
and that is more than I deserve,
He has blessings stored up for me
in Heavenly reserves.
It's not because of who I am or anything that I've done,
It's because of Jesus, God's righteous Holy Son.
Jesus intercedes to the Father on my behalf,
Because of this intercession, I am spared God's wrath.
If it had not been for His blood,
I would justly be condemned,
But because of the price Jesus paid,
I've been forgiven of my sins.
There is no doubt that Jesus lives,
It's evident in the daily grace,
mercies, and blessings He gives.

Pray

Though your days seem dark,
And you feel like you have lost your spark.
Every day you struggle to cope,
Remember this, there is always hope.
Money is short and the month is long,
It's harder now that your spouse is gone.
You feel like throwing in the towel,
You need to know things will get better in a little while.
You are raising your children all by yourself,
And you are struggling with failing health.
You wonder how you will make ends meet,
Hang in there, never accept defeat.
A few words of wisdom for you to hear,
Remember God is always near.
He hears every word you say,
It's time to fall on your knees and pray.
The Lord can supply your every need,
Trust in Him and sincerely believe.
I know the Lord will make a way,
All you have to do is pray.

Remember the Call

Let the anointing of the Lord fall fresh and new,
Remember what we've been commissioned to do.
We weren't called to be spiritually filled
and not share with others,
We were called to impart the gospel
to our unsaved sisters and brothers.
So many yearn to receive the truth,
Not only the old but also the youth.
Thirsty people on the broad path to hell,
Unwittingly passing by God's everlasting,
life-giving well.
They will never know unless they are taught,
They won't be found unless they are sought.
Harvest time is now,
There is so much work to do.
Since the laborers are few,
It's up to me and you.
God's word must go forth,
To every person on the earth.
To all saints this task was given,
We must remain focused and driven.
Witnessing to broken souls,
Sharing the gospel that can make them whole.

Rescued

The way I lived my life not so long ago,
I had no direction and wondered which way to go.
Searching but never finding what I was looking for,
Knowing that there had to be something better in store.
There was a constant knocking at the door of my heart,
But I was afraid to answer because
I feared a brand-new start.
Even though I loathed the wretched state that I was in,
But like a pig in mud, I wallowed in sin.
My flesh told me if it felt good it surely must be right,
Soon the darkness set in and
dimmed the precious light.
Deeper and deeper I descended
with seemingly no way out,
Constant ignoring the voice inside
telling me I've taken the wrong route.
As time went on, I began to feel lost,
I struggled in a mad cold world filled with chaos.

My rope was burning on both ends,
with only inches left,
I felt like I was drowning, fighting for one last breath.
I was at the crossroads and had to make a decision,
Running toward destruction,
facing an imminent collision.
I stopped what I was doing and fell down on my knees,
I cried out, "Jesus, will you help me please!
Have mercy on me, Lord, I want to live.
I repent for my sins, will you please forgive."
All of a sudden with the gentleness of a dove,
The Lord showered me with
unspeakable peace and love.
From then to now I've not been the same,
I'm saved in Jesus' name.

Struggling

This journey's not easy,
You never said that it would be.
Now that I'm on the right track,
Satan's trying to pull me back.
Temptation is on every hand,
Lord, I need You to stand.
Because in this world of sin,
I find myself struggling.
I'm doing all I can,
To live according to your plan.
It seems the closer I get to You,
The more trials that I go through.
I need You to make me strong,
Lord, please help me to carry on.
Because time and time again,
I find myself struggling.
Doing wrong is easy,
Sometimes it's hard to do right.

The Holy Spirit says walk away,
The flesh says stay and fight.
There's a battle deep within,
Trying to knock me back into sin.
Lord, I'm trying to make it in,
But I confess to You that I'm struggling.
I can't give up,
I won't give in,
I've come too far,
To start again.
I think of what You've done for me,
With you is where I want to be.
Lord, on You I do depend,
To help me while I'm struggling.
Oh Lord, I'm struggling but
I'm pressing through to the end.

Woman of Favor

The favor of the Lord rests upon you,
You are blessed in all you do.
It's time for you to understand,
That you've been touched by God's hand.
His touch ensures your success,
It guarantees His joy, peace, and happiness.
If you abide by the Creator's will,
His promises to you will be fulfilled.
God chose you and set you apart,
To serve others with a humble heart.
To be effective in the service you provide,
Conceit and pride must be set aside.
Let the light of God's spirit shine brightly through,
Stay on the course that God has set for you.
Walk with other Women of Favor,
Those who exemplify godly behavior.
Avoid those filled with negativity,
They'll drain all of your positive energy.
Continue to walk upright in the footsteps
of our Lord the Savior,
Demonstrating the characteristics of a Woman of Favor.

You Can Make It

You might be stressed, depressed,
Down to your last dime.
All your bills are due,
You don't know how you'll make it through.
You're raising your kids all alone,
And all your hope is gone.
Hold on to Jesus and never let go.
The doctor may have told you,
There's nothing he can do.
That you won't make it through,
And it has got you feeling hopeless, sad, and blue.
Or maybe your child is running wild,
Completely gone astray.
It seems like you'll never see the light of day.
I'm here to tell you,
Jesus can see you through.
Never ever doubt,
That He can work it out.
Don't give up,
Don't give in,
Depend on Jesus until the end.
You can make it,
With Jesus, you can make it.

He Will Be Your Light

Grandma said troubles won't last,
They too will have to pass.
For a while the clouds will hover,
Blocking rays of hope like a dark, black, wool cover.
Thoughts of what ifs and what might happen
Loom in the back of my mind.
While I'm in a battle trying to find
Peace in the midst of the storm,
"Give up, throw in the towel,"
An unfamiliar voice whispers in my ear.
"It's not worth your trouble,
You are the loser in this struggle,
There is no way that you can win,
I will destroy your child in the end.
I've caused great men of God to fall,
Just like them, your child has
answered me when I called."

I told the devil that in the name of Jesus, he must flee,
He will never have anyone in my family.
The grip he has is about to be broken,
Salvation, life, blessings,
and deliverance are now being spoken.
In the name of Jesus, I claim victory,
God is in control and my child is now free.
Gone are all the demonic burdens
that weighed my child down,
The mercies of the Lord are abundantly abounding.
This is a promise from the Lord
on which we all can depend,
The devil will be destroyed in the end.
The winds might be blowing with hurricane force,
It is imperative that we all stay on the right course.
Soon night will be over and the storms will cease,
With the daylight comes an unspeakable peace.
To the Savior's everlasting arm, hold on tight,
He will be your light in the darkness of the night.

Oh, The Joy I Have!

Thank you Heavenly Father for your grace and mercy,
Without You, my existence would be filled with misery.
Oh, the joy I have!
I rest peacefully in Your loving arms,
You shelter me from all evil, danger, hurt, and harm.
In reverence of You I bow on bended knees,
Humbly giving thanks for the blessings
You've bestowed upon me.
Oh, the joy I have!
My confidence lies in thee and thee alone,
You have breathed life into my dead, dry bones.
Majestic and mighty, holy creator of all,
Jesus! Jesus! Jesus!
Demons tremble when your name is called.
Oh, the joy I have!
Knowing that the devil is already defeated,
Soon You'll return and Your mission will be completed.
Glory, adoration, and praise belong only to You, Lord,
I love to worship You with my spiritual sisters
and brothers on one accord.
Oh, the joy I have!
I take comfort in the blessed assurance
that You have given,
I rejoice in the fact that by the blood
of Jesus my sins are forgiven.
Oh, the joy I have!

Praise the Creator

I was created for a purpose,
According to His will,
Believe me when I tell you,
The God I serve is real.
He called me out of darkness,
Now I can plainly see,
That without His grace and mercy,
There would be no hope for me.
I know Him for myself,
He is my Lord and King,
The God of all creation,
He is my everything.
I had to let you know,
About all that God has done,
Give praises to the only wise God,
Each and everyone.

The Greatest Gift of All

To God be the glory,
Praise His holy name,
Righteous and Almighty,
I'm grateful that He came.
I've received many gifts,
Some big and some small,
But Jesus the Risen Savior,
Was truly the greatest gift of all.
God chose His only son,
To come down to earth.
Mary, the blessed virgin,
Gave the Savior birth.
Wrapped in swaddling clothes,
The scriptures do recall,
Jesus the Lord and Savior,
Was the greatest gift of all.
So many gifts are given,
This season and throughout the year,
For very special occasions,
To loved ones far and near.
Beautifully wrapped,
Filled with items from the mall,
But Jesus the Lord and Savior,
Is truly the greatest gift of all.

Willing Vessel

In order for me to be what God wants me to be,
I have to start believing in me,
Recognize my God-given capabilities,
Consider all the possibilities,
Consult God on everything I do,
Because only God can see me through.
I can't let people with negative opinions and views,
Keep me from what God wants me to do.
To the Lord I'll forever stay true,
I'll be a willing vessel that He can use.

The Treasures of Your Heart ... Where Are They?

Way down deep in the heart a treasure chest hides,
Only God and you know the contents inside.
The things valued the most reside there,
Things we treat gently, with extra love and care.
A treasure is something we keep guarded,
A treasure is so special it can't be discarded.
"Where your treasure is, there will your heart be also,"
Luke 12:34 plainly states,
Time for a heart checkup, time to self-evaluate.
Some of our treasure chests are
brimming full and overflowing,
Some things have slipped inside
without us even knowing.
There are some who treasure things
like money, power, fortune, and fame,
While others treasure the status and position
associated with their last name.

Looks, beauty, and image
are highly treasured by some,
But what happens when old age
sets in and the wrinkles come?
Material things like houses, cars, clothes, purses,
and shoes are treasured by many,
To attain those things, folks fall deep into
credit card debt because they spent their last penny.
Unequally yoked relationships with men
are treasured and can become all-consuming,
Seek God for a husband because
wolves in sheep clothing are very unassuming.
A relationship with Jesus Christ is the
most precious and greatest treasure one can possess,
It is everlasting and unique, unlike all the rest.
Esteem the Lord as your most valued treasure,
make Him the King of your heart today,
Then you will receive a heavenly treasure
that never fails or passes away.

Taming the Tongue

Sticks and stones may break bones,
Reckless words can break a spirit.
Hurtful words leave invisible wounds
that sometimes never heal,
Consider how your words will make a person feel.
Words have the power to lift up and also tear down,
Mean words can instantly turn a smile into a frown.
Hateful words can incite a violent, uncontrollable riot,
There is a time to speak and also a time to just be quiet.
Too often, without thinking, we speak,
We say the wrong things,
We don't hold our peace,
We refuse to be Christ-like and turn the other cheek.
At times we are too proud to simply walk away,
Instead we make a foolish decision
and in arrogance we stay.
Arguments sometimes turn into a fight,
Negativity displayed by Christians
dims the Savior's light.
We need the Holy Ghost to keep our tongues tamed,
Our tongues are as unruly as a wildfire's flame.
We make it perfectly clear that
at any cost we will be heard,
In our minds, an issue cannot be resolved
unless we have the last word.
Father God, in Jesus' name, please hear us as we pray,
We need Your help to tame our tongues
each and every day.
Remind us daily that at all times we represent You,
Help us to glorify You with every word we say
and in everything we do.
Amen.

Women Striving for Excellence in Times Like These

We live in perilous times,
The news is filled with reports of diseases,
wars, natural disasters, failing economies,
and horrific crimes.
But we will keep our minds on Jesus
and He will keep us in perfect peace,
We are women striving for excellence
in times like these.
We have let go of the past and left it behind,
We were saved by grace and given renewed minds.
We are Godly examples in our homes,
our churches, and our communities,
We are women striving for excellence
in times like these.
We walk in God's will and not our own,
We stand for what is right and denounce what is wrong.
We are motivated by love and
not by selfishness or greed,

We are women striving for excellence
in times like these.
We have been taught how to mature the Christ within,
God's word teaches us how to live holy
and free from sin.
We have been equipped with all the tools that we need,
We are women striving for excellence
in times like these.
We will not be distracted by the trouble in the land,
We will continue to live according
to God's purpose and plan.
We will think on what is true, noble, right, pure,
lovely, admirable, excellent, and praiseworthy,
Because we are women striving for excellence
in times like these.

Now That I'm Saved

Now that I'm saved,
I don't go to the club no more,
I don't drink and don't smoke no more,
I don't cuss and don't act like a fool,
I don't do the wrong that I used to do.
Now that I'm saved,
I treat everybody right,
I compromise instead of fuss and fight,
Now I see what I couldn't see,
No longer bound, I've been set free.
Now that I'm saved,
I talk that Jesus talk,
I walk like Jesus walked,
I praise the Savior's name,
I have stopped doing the same old same.
Now that I'm saved,
I pray for those who hate on me,
I help those who are in need,
Daily God's word I study and read,
And I pray continuously.
Now that I'm saved,
I've got the victory,
Joy replaced misery,
I walk in His marvelous light,
Jesus is the head of my life.

Don't Throw in the Towel!

Troubles kicked down the door
and disturbed the peace,
Trials kept coming and refused to cease.
Dazed and confused, lying on the ground,
Then God whispered to me, "Don't throw in the towel!"

"One! two!" the devil began to shout,
God said, "You are down but not out!"
With a loud voice the devil cried, "Three!"
God told the devil, "This one belongs to me."

God whispered this promise in my ear,
"I will never leave or forsake you, my dear."
The devil declared, "She will not survive,"
As he pounded the ground and screamed, "Four! five!"

God's promise strengthened me
and I got off the ground,
I refused to let the devil keep me bound and down.
I am more than a conqueror through Him who loves me,
In the name of Jesus, I declare victory.

Jesus is our loving savior, our everlasting friend,
In the midst of life's storms, on Him we can depend.
So, when the trials of life try to keep you down,
Remember God's promises
and *don't throw in the towel!*

In Times Like These We Need a Savior

In times like these we need a Savior, to take us by the hand, to lead and guide us because there is a relentless enemy who has invaded our land. The enemy has enticed many saints to fall away, led astray by their own worldly desires instead of adhering to God's salvation plan. The truth is that without a Savior we will not be able to stand.

In times like these we need a Savior, to breathe the breath of life back into our lifeless, dry bones, to shake us up and remove the spirit of complacency, to reignite our souls on fire so the church can once again be the beacon of hope in our communities.

In times like these we need a Savior, to imitate and
demonstrate His obedient behavior. When we were
saved, we were given a job to do, to spread the
gospel to a dying world. Time is winding down.
We have to let sinners know to seek
the Lord while He can be found.
The harvest remains plentiful and even though
churches are packed, still the laborers are few.
Lord, please give us the desire to do
what You have commissioned us to do.

In times like these we need a Savior, because there
are clouds of wickedness and deception hovering all
over the world. Look at the legislation recently passed,
designed to corrupt the minds of school-aged boys and
girls. What used to be wrong, society now calls right.
It's time for the church to take a stand and fight.
We have to hold up Christ's blood-stained banner
and let His light break through those clouds
and forever shine bright.
Jesus is the Savior. He is the only way.
In times like these we need the Savior,
more and more each day.

Breaking Up Our Fallow Ground Is Hard to Do

Look in the mirror.
Are you satisfied with who is staring back at you?
The truth be told, we all have some breaking up to do.
One who is lacking in character is one who is shallow,
God's word instructs us to
break up ground that is fallow.
Breaking up ground is hard to do
and oh so painfully true.

In this life we have been given a patch
of fertile ground to toil,
But over the years we have neglected our soil.
Now the ground has become overrun
with weeds that have to be removed,
Our ground has become fallow and
breaking it up will be hard to do.

The weeds have choked the life
out of the fruits of the spirit,
Some of our ground has become so unsightly
that no one wants to go near it.
Let's put on our gloves, there is work to do.
It's time to become a better me and a better you.

We need to ask God for discernment
and to make us aware,

So that we can weed out everything
in our lives that should not be there.
We must pull out every single weed,
plucking them from the root,
This might be unpleasant because
we might discover a few ugly truths.
Snatch out weeds of low self-esteem,
hurt, guilt, lies, jealousy, insecurity,
Fear, addiction, fornication, resentment,
envy, and gossiping, just to name a few.
Remember, breaking up is not easy, it is hard to do.

We are all flawed so no one
can point a judgmental finger,
Even as saints, the specters of our pasts
will always linger,
Trying to knock us back to where we used to be,
But when that happens, resist the devil and he will flee.

Let the word of God be our plow,
The time for breaking up our fallow ground is now.
Stay focused and committed to daily righteous living,
Be mindful of the call that we all have been given.
Let us recommit ourselves to Jesus Christ today,
So that we will not be deceived and led astray.
Daily study God's word to be reminded
of His promises and truths,
Plant seeds of righteousness and
love to reap the spirit's fruits.
In order to reap the fullness of the joy
that God freely gives,
We have to break up our fallow ground
and change the way we live.

River of Life

The river of life runs too fast,
I try hard to keep up.
Its waters are inviting,
But too cold to enjoy.
There are so many obstacles in the river's path,
I must be mindful of all the twists
and turns on this river's course.
If I stay on task, I will successfully make it to the end,
But on the riverbanks are so many enticing things,
They beckon me to divert and get off track.
I take a long hard look and count up the cost.
If I fall by the wayside and indulge
in the wonders that I see,
I might not finish my trek.
So, I choose to not partake.
My mind is fixed,
No time to waver.
On this journey down the river of life,
I will reach my final destination—Heaven.
It's not always a smooth sail,
Sometimes the winds will blow and the rains will fall,
I remain encouraged because I know
the Lord Almighty is there through it all,
As I travel down the river of life.

Changed

I grabbed the hand stretched out to me,
Once bound but now free.
Walking in light,
Darkness is gone.
Feelings of love,
A part of a family,
Now I belong.
All this is new,
Never felt before,
As each day passes,
There's more in store.
Happiness and inner peace achieved,
This for me, who would have believed?
Everyone gave up on me,
And so did I.
Down so low,
I prayed, *God, please let me die.*
But just as the last tear fell from my eye,
I heard a voice from out of the sky.
Startled, I began to shake,
The ground I stood on began to quake.
"Are you sure you want your life to end?"
the voice did say,
"For if it does, today will be your Judgment Day.

You haven't accepted my Son Jesus
or asked for your sins to be forgiven,
And I have kept records on how you've been living.
You won't enter Heaven's eternal gate,
Hell will be your certain fate.
If you really want me to proceed with your plan,
I will strike you down, right where you stand.
But if you want a chance to make things right,
Repent and you'll be made new this very night."
I fell to my knees and began to pray,
God, please don't take my life away.
I accept Jesus as my Lord and Savior,
Forgive my sins and ungodly behavior.
Tonight, I want to begin again.
My trust, I put only in thee,
Please loosen the devil's hold and set me free.
The voice said your sins are now erased,
All addictions and strongholds are gone,
I'll strengthen you to carry on.
There'll be more valleys to go through,
But remember I have a purpose for you.
Never let go of my unchanging hand,
Live life anew according to My divine plan.
You are now changed in Jesus' name.

Let Go and Leave the Past Behind

You say Heaven is your goal,
And there is nothing worth losing your soul.
Still you continue to look back,
You constantly get off track.
Once you fully commit to Christ in your heart and mind,
You will be able to let go and leave the past behind.
The life you once led is over and done,
You've been saved by grace through
the blood of Jesus, God's Holy Son.
It doesn't matter how you used to live,
When you confessed and repented,
God loved you enough to forget and forgive.
So, all the guilt and shame that linger in your mind,
Let go and leave the past behind.
Holding on to the past can ruin your life,
Remember Lot's Wife?
Thoughts of yesterday flooded her mind,
She couldn't let go and leave her past behind.
For her disobedience she paid the ultimate cost,
When she looked back, her life was instantly lost.
It's time to pray and seek God's face,
To get rooted in His word and grow in His grace.
Stop letting the storm winds knock you down,
Let the word of God strengthen you
and keep you off the ground.
With a clean heart and a renewed mind,
Let go and leave the past behind.

Reminders from Our Heavenly Father

My child, I promise to never leave your side,
I'll keep you safe from harm and
all your needs will be supplied.
When times get tough and it's hard to stand,
Reach out and grab my unfailing hand.
I'll be your guide if you allow me to,
I'll always see you safely through.
Everyday won't be sunny; at times there will be rain,
And when your heart is heavy,
don't forget that there is a purpose in your pain.
Remember the grace and mercy that I freely give,
You shall be blessed as long as you shall live.
I knew you long before the day of your birth,
My love for you goes further
than the deepest depths of earth.

You're no accident nor are you a mistake,
there's a reason why you're here,
Just talk to me and read my word,
then your purpose will be clear.
The death and resurrection of your big brother Jesus
made all things possible for you,
My Holy Spirit will give you strength
to accomplish what you've been called to do.
Be sure to love all of your sisters and brothers,
just as I love you,
Remember, I am watching everything you do.
One day I will call you to come and be with me,
Then we will be together throughout eternity.
Love,
Your Heavenly Father

Forgiveness

The Tree of Forgiveness produces life-giving fruit
and everyone should try it,
Forgiveness should be an essential part
of our spiritual diets.
God, the Father of Forgiveness,
planted the Forgiveness Tree,
The power of forgiveness sets the soul free.
Forgiveness stomps out anger's raging flames,
Forgiveness leaves us with no one to blame.
Forgiveness sweetens and softens a bitter soul,
Forgiveness can warm a heart that is icy cold.
Forgiveness produces love, not hate,
Forgiveness replaces a grudge with grace.
Forgiveness can mend a broken heart,
Forgiveness offers a dying relationship
a brand-new start.
Forgiveness gently calms a troubled mind,
Forgiveness allows the past to be left behind.
Forgiveness silences a slanderous tongue
and makes foolish arguments cease,
Forgiveness is the key to happiness, joy, and peace.
Father God, thank you for the forgiveness of our sins,
Help us as we search our hearts and look deep within.
Bring to mind any unforgiveness that may be found,
Lord, we no longer want to be bound.
Help us to forgive those
who have caused us hurt and pain,
We realize that forgiveness must be given
before it can be gained.
Father, I ask this in Jesus' name.
Amen.

Commit to the Harvest

God is mighty and God is great,
because of His faithfulness today we celebrate.
Jubilare Evangelistic Ministries would not exist today
if it had not been a part of God's perfect plan.
Thank God for entrusting this place of worship
in our pastor's hands.
It took faith and courage to bring the vision
that God gave our pastor into fruition 26 years ago.
With amazement we have witnessed
how God has blessed and allowed Jubilare to grow.
Continued outreach is what we are striving to do.
But like Matthew 9:37 says,
"The harvest is plentiful but the workers are few."
To Christians the commission was given
to spread the gospel of Christ Jesus.
We have to be willing to let the Lord use us.
Just coming to church, getting fed God's word, and not
sharing it with others is not why God has us here.
I challenge each saved member of Jubilare
to share the gospel of Jesus Christ
with at least five people this year.
Our pastor and teachers continually
give us all the tools that we need.
We don't have to be afraid to witness,
just let the Lord take the lead.
If we are serious, God will place someone in our way.
He will give us the exact words to say.
All we have to do is our part.
God is the only one who touches and changes hearts.
So, let's honor God by giving Him our best as we
commit to being workers in the plentiful harvest.

Please Keep Walking in Your Deliverance

Let go and leave the past behind,
Let God's word fill your heart and your mind.
Keep moving forward,
Stop looking back,
The devil is on a mission trying to get you off track.
Please keep walking in your deliverance.
It's not the time to throw in the towel,
You might be discouraged,
but things will be better after a while.
This journey gets tough,
But God is there with you,
Trust in the Unlimited God
to see you all the way through.
Please keep walking in your deliverance.
You've been saved, delivered, and set free,
Stand firm in your faith,
Let rivers of thankfulness flow from your heart,
As you praise the Lord for a fresh start.
Continue to live your life in Him,
Please keep walking in your deliverance.

The Holy Ghost will keep you if you allow Him to,
Don't override the spirit when he tells you what to do.
Pray for wisdom and discernment,
Keep God's armor on and
stay ready for a spiritual fight,
Let God's presence be the light
in the dark places of your life.
Please keep walking in your deliverance.

Sistah Saint

I'm not saved, but one day I hope to be,
Until I make it in, I pray God has mercy on me.
I go to church sometimes, each time I see you there.
Shouting and praising God like you are truly on fire,
The last time I went, you were singing in the choir.
I guess you forgot to close your window last night,
I heard you cussing and arguing
in the middle of a fight.
I don't care what you do, but I have this complaint,
How could such vile words come from
the mouth of a woman named *Sistah Saint?*
I saw him, your frequent late-night visitor,
creeping out of your house,
Tiptoeing down the driveway, quiet as a mouse,
Late last night, or should I say early this morning,
This isn't the first time and I'm sure it won't be the last.
I don't care what you do, but I have this complaint,
How could you fornicate and do such things
when your name is *Sistah Saint?*

You walked right passed me,
With your nose high in the air,
Caught up with your friends, you didn't notice me there.
At first, I thought it strange
that you were in the same place as me,
Because this is where I go
when I want to chill and be totally free.
I drink and get a buzz and dance until dawn,
And when my favorite song comes on,
I can't help but sing along.
I don't care what you do, but I have this complaint,
How could you party harder than me
when your name is *Sistah Saint?*
Your testimony is flawed,
I see you as a fake,
I hope you get right for your own soul's sake.
Where is the Holy Fire that you claim the Savior lit?
Sistah Saint, you discourage others
by being a hypocrite.

Preparation for Spiritual Warfare

Don't be fooled, the devil is real
and his power is strong,
So, it is imperative that in these last and evil days
we keep the whole armor of God on.
The devil's mission is to destroy, kill, and steal,
He wants the true gospel of Jesus Christ
to be concealed.
Old Satan has so many tricks up his wicked sleeves,
Without the full armor of God, we will be deceived.
Those who have been defeated
entered the battle unprepared,
There are steps that must be taken
to be victorious in spiritual warfare.
First, true commitment to the Lord must be declared,
Without Jesus Christ we will not win,
no matter how much we prepare.
We have to be ready in order to stand,
So, put on the whole armor of God
and follow His battle plan.

If we keep our minds on the Lord,
then perfect peace we will find,
We can't enter the battle with
a confused and troubled mind.
It's time to get focused, turn off social media and the tv;
let's get back to the Bible, God's Holy Word,
Too much of that worldly mess can get
our spiritual perspective distorted and blurred.
Put on the whole armor of God, your battle gear,
Prepare to drive Satan away from here.
If you are tired of being bombarded
by the enemies' fire,
Cry out to the Lord and lift the name of Jesus higher.
We'll use praise as our secret weapon
and the Bible as our sword,
We will draw a line in the sand and
begin to execute our battle plan.

The Final Call (Selah)

The angel of the Lord spoke on His behalf,
He came to give warning of what would come to pass.
Because of God's mercy,
sinners were given one last chance.
To the inhabitants of the earth the angel warned:
Trouble is coming,
Worse than mankind has ever seen.
Earth is on the brink of disaster,
And it is closer than you think.
The time is now to accept Jesus as Lord of all.
Tomorrow may be too late,
Don't continue in your sins and let death seal your fate.
Woe unto those whose hearts have been hardened,
All who repent will be forever pardoned.
I was sent here this day to give the final call,
To extend God's salvation invitation
not to one but to all.
This is now the appointed hour,
Don't let it pass you by.

The Most High God

In the splendor of your holiness, I bow before you Lord,
I offer praises and thanksgiving
to the Creator of the world.
Jubilant is my spirit, filled with your precious love,
Wondrous are your blessings
that rain from Heaven above.
God of all gods, all power is in your hands,
The glory of your being is present in every land.
You alone are worthy to receive the highest praise,
Today, tomorrow, forever, and always.

www.ingramcontent.com/pod-product-compliance
Lightning Source LLC
Chambersburg PA
CBHW022021290426
44109CB00015B/1264